100 Good Reasons to Stay Single

... and Be Proud of It!

You have the bed all to yourself.

And you can sleep like a king, starfish style.

You can talk to your dog like a buddy.
And he never interrupts you.

You can eat pizza seven nights in a row.
No one saying "Again?"

You can leave the toilet paper on the living room table.

Who's going to judge you?

No one steals your duvet at night.

Or wakes you up for a "chat" (= an argument) at 2 AM.

You have 100% control of the remote.

Yes, even to binge football matches or action movies.

You can sing off-key in the shower.
And pretend you're Freddie Mercury (or Elvis Presley) without shame.

No need to share your beer.

Or your chips. Or your fries. Nothing at all.

No one criticizes your weird playlist.

Yes, even if it switches from Booba to Céline Dion.

You can go on a weekend trip with your friends on a whim.

No need to ask permission.

Your bank account is yours alone.
No gifts to buy for your mother-in-law (phew!).

You can lounge around in your boxers all day.
And no one complains.

No "When are you coming home?" texts.

You can come back at 5 AM relaxed. Or even later.

You can sleep with 4 pillows and 2 duvets. Or completely naked.

No complaints about it being too hot or cold.

No endless meals at the in-laws.

Your Sunday = couch + FIFA.

You can eat garlic and onions at every meal.
No conflicts caused.

Your favorite snacks are safe.

No one secretly eats them.

No obligation to watch a romantic movie.
You can watch Die Hard for the 12th time.

**You can adopt a dog...
or an iguana...**
No one says "That's a bad idea!"

You can take up the whole couch.
And fall asleep diagonally on it.

Your mismatched socks? No one notices.

And frankly, you don't care.

You can leave your stuff everywhere.

No comments about the "mess."

No long discussions at night.
Just you and Netflix.

No fuss about the dishes.

If it's dirty, it's you. And you don't care.

You can dance in your boxers in your living room.
No one's filming (thankfully).

No one hogs your phone.
Or snoops your messages (whew!).

You can set the AC however you want.

Your comfort > everything else.

No need to compromise on decor.

Yes to car and superhero posters... and manga figurines!

You can skip Valentine's Day guilt-free.

And save up for a PS6.

No debates about what movie to watch.
YOU decide.

You can change your life plans tomorrow.
No one to hold you back.

You can eat in bed without complaints.
The crumbs? Your problem.

No birthdays to remember.
Your brain says "Thanks."

You can move to Australia tomorrow.
No one to stop you.

You can keep a chaotic lifestyle.
Go to bed at 3 AM? Wake up at noon? No problem!

You can flirt with whoever you want.
No accountability.

No jealousy fits.
Zero drama.

You can put your phone on airplane mode.

And no one panics. Maybe except your mom?

You can eat stinky cheese.

No "That smells like a corpse" comments.

No scary texts like "We need to talk..."
Absolute peace.

You can hit on the waitress.

Or just smile at her. Chill.

You can binge-watch South Park, The Simpsons, or One Piece.

No complaints.

You can sign up for MMA or pottery classes.

No debates.

No one monopolizes the bathroom.
The shower is yours.

You can leave the fridge empty... or full of beers.

Your priorities.

You can eat pasta for 3 weeks straight.
No sighs at the table.

You can keep your old, holey t-shirt.
No judgment.

You can cry watching Rocky III.
So what?

You can sleep diagonally on the king-size bed.
With your two dogs if you want.

You can eat chips for breakfast.
No "You're eating that?" looks.

You can repaint your apartment black and red.

No eye rolls.

You can spend an hour in the bath with a beer.
No waiting lines.

You can scroll Tinder... just for laughs.
Or not ;)

You can keep your curtains closed all weekend.

Cave mode activated.

You can keep your beard Viking style.
Zero comments.

You can let Netflix ask "One more episode?"
Yes, always!

You can buy silly gadgets on Amazon or AliExpress.
It's YOUR money.

You can burp without saying sorry.
No ears bleeding.

You can redecorate every 10 years.
Maybe.

You can nap after breakfast.

No one judges.

You can cook pork ribs at midnight.

It's your house.

You can dress as Spider-Man at home.

No one judges.

You can fart freely in your living room.
No need to blame the dog.

You can play FIFA for 12 hours straight.

No "You spend too much time on that!" complaints.

You can have a solo raclette night in July.
Because you want to.

You can keep the same sheet for 3 weeks.
No complaints.

You can go out in sweatpants and flip-flops.
Zero pressure.

You can buy an $800 electric scooter.
No one says it's stupid.

You can invite whoever you want for a gaming night.
No approval needed.

You can eat an XXL burger at 2 AM.
No comments on your eating habits.

You can keep the console plugged in all the time.
No complaints about the "ugly decor."

You can sleep in your jeans if you're too lazy to change.

Who will know?

You can leave your place a mess.
No one asks you to vacuum.

You can drink Coke for breakfast.
No "That's unhealthy" remarks.

You can watch fail compilations on YouTube for 3 hours.

Zero judgment.

You can sleep with the TV on.
No "That keeps me awake" complaints.

You can work on your abs... or just think about it.

No one yells at you for being lazy.

You can store 30 beers in the fridge.

No need to leave room for veggies.

You can leave your socks lying around the living room.
They're comfy there.

You can buy a motorcycle without negotiation.
Just because it makes you happy.

You can sleep with the window open in winter.

No complaints about the cold.

You can leave the toilet paper on the living room table.

Who's going to judge you?

You can wear the same jeans 7 days straight.

If it doesn't smell, it's fine.

You can never fold your laundry.
The chair becomes a wardrobe.

You can eat straight from the pan or container.

Less dishes, more fun.

You can buy a 75-inch TV without justification.
It's an investment.

You can sleep with your old favorite football t-shirt.

Even if it has holes.

You can spend 4 hours playing GTA.

No "Your game again?!" complaints.

You can leave dirty dishes in the sink for 3 days.

No one complains.

You can decorate your place with football jerseys.

It's a masculine art gallery.

You can shave your head on a whim.
No panic to manage.

You can eat a whole pack of Haribo.
Zero sharing.

You can leave empty cans as decoration.

Industrial loft vibe.

You can have 5 consoles plugged in at once.

It's your museum.

You can wear the same sweatshirt 4 days in a row.
No complaints.

You can sing Johnny while doing the dishes.

Or not do them at all.

You can sleep on the couch because you want to.
No need to justify.

You can have breakfast at 4 PM.
Or cook a steak at 2 AM.

You can have a messy beard all the time.
It's the urban grizzly style.

You can stay single and happy.
Because you're already whole.

Printed in Dunstable, United Kingdom

75471508R00058